# Chivalry Is Not Dead: Boston

A Modern Gentleman's Guide to Planning a Classic Date

## By Adrien Saporiti

Chivalry is Not Dead:
Boston

A Modern Gentleman's Guide to Planning a Classic Date

By:
Adrien Saporiti

Edited By:
Laura Dabrowski
Adrien Saporiti

Photo:
Shawn Lemon

Cover Design:
Adrien Saporiti

ISBN- 978-0-9840572-8-3

Library of Congress
© 2011 Thumbs Up Publishing.

Printed in the United States & England, available in ebooks and on the iBookstore.

## Dedication

This book is dedicated to Laura, Kirsten, and Becky, for putting the idea in my head and championing this project, even when I forgot about it.

# About the Author

## ADRIEN SAPORITI

Adrien Saporiti is a Nashville, TN native, raised to be a true Southern gentleman. He wears several hats, including those of musician, artist, and now, author. Having spent his collegiate years in Boston, Adrien attended the Berklee College of Music where he studied everything from arranging to film scoring. A close group of female friends, personal experiences, and intimate knowledge of the city developed over those years helped form the concept of "Chivalry is not Dead." Currently based out of Nashville and Boston, Adrien spends the rest of his time traveling the country writing books, making art, and playing music.

**www.chivalryinboston.com**

If you're interested in checking out Adrien's music and seeing some of his art, visit:

**WWW.WATERLOOCREATIVE.COM**

**The author thanks his family, the Krahn family, Ross Bresler, all of the young women who have been kind enough to date him and Wellesley College.**

# TABLE OF CONTENTS

# About This Book

In college I was the guy who hung out with a lot of girls. I didn't date or sleep with all of them, most of them were just really good friends. The downside to this was that I missed a lot of opportunities because girls would see me out with a friend and think we were already on a date. The upside was that I came up with a lot of great ideas for dates while out as a friend. I learned that experiences are everything, and flash is minimal.

Planning a date doesn't have to be a production, but it should have some thought behind it. A lot of my guy friends would get really excited for their date, but then always end up pulling from the same grab bag of dates they always did. If you're going to ask a girl out you should plan something that shows you're actually excited to be there with her. It doesn't take much, just a little pre-planning. That's where this book comes in.

It can be hard coming up with a good date on your own. The lines between trite, original, and tried-too-hard are painfully thin,which is why I compiled my best dates in this book. They're probably not what might come to mind right away when planning a date, and that's the point. There are a variety of different ideas that cover a lot of Boston, and a lot of them are adaptable to whatever location works for you. I came up with these ideas from dates I went on or from friend dates, and the reason they work is because they're all things you could do with a friend and they'd still be the fun. That's the trick. You may click, and you may not. But if you take the weight off and approach it like you're just going to hang out, at least you'll have a good time.

So take these ideas, do the leg work and forethought required of a good date, and make it yours. You don't have to tell her I'm providing you with the idea, because you're making it happen.

*DISCLAIMER: This is not a book to help you hookup with girls. If it happens, then count yourself lucky, don't be a jerk, and at least take her on another date.*

# Guide to being a Good Date

**Listen:** From the time you ask your date out to the second date and beyond, no other skill will serve you better. If she mentions anything about herself, it's worth remembering. How many siblings, her best friend's name, her roommate's name, etc., all worth remembering. The more you can remember shows the more you were paying attention and lets her know, 'Hey, this guy is really interested." Listen with sincere interest and you'll be rewarded. Promise.

**Preparation:** Being prepared is the difference between a fantastic date and the worst night of your life. If you're trying to impress someone it's much more impressive if it seems like you know what you're doing. Here's a few examples of what I'm talking about:

- **Know where you're going. We've got Google Maps now, so no excuse.**
- **Have alternatives in case you have to improvise.**
- **Call to confirm the date, and when you do:**
- **Let her know what to be prepared for (as an example), If you're going to be outside a lot, let her know to dress warmly.**
- **If you're cooking for her or going out to dinner, ask about food allergies. If you want to be discreet you can say "Are there any foods you don't like?"**
- **Check the weather and be prepared for it (ie - umbrella).**

**Etiquette:** Most guys don't follow proper etiquette these days, so doing so is like an automatic leg-up for you. See the etiquette section for some basic rules on modern dating etiquette.

**Be on Time:** Being on time shows respect. I guarantee you most girls aren't use to this.

**Sincerity is Key:** In the forced pseudo-intimate social situation that is dating all senses are heightened, on both sides. Girls can smell insincerity the way animals smell fear, so stay focussed on your date and what she's saying (ie- listen), and respond honestly.

*Trick:* If she really is boring try listening to her words the way you would a foreign language, by focusing on key words. Keeping yourself focused on keywords will force you to listen, at least long enough to get through the date. Bonus, if she ever senses your disinterest you'll be able to prove her wrong. Well, sort of.

**Be Adaptable, Be Observant:** Even if you've chosen the perfect date, prepped and planned it to the T (no pun intended), it's probably not always going to go according to plan. That can be a good thing though, so try and find a way to use it to your advantage. A waiter spills a drink on you? Try and turn it into a joke. The concert got cancelled? Grab some speakers, go down to the Charles, and listen to the band via your iPod. Girls are like kids, as long as you stay cool and enjoy yourself, they will too.

**Appearance:** We all want a girl to like us for who we are and that includes how we dress. I agree, but I don't think that means we can completely neglect appearance all together. I'm not saying "suit up", unless you are in fact a bro who already suits up. In which case, awesome. But just the basic showering, grooming, and picking out a clean outfit that doesn't have too many holes in it will do. Girls go to great lengths to look stunning for us and then pretend like it's no big deal. The least we can do is iron a shirt, right?

**Don't try and be smooth, You're not:** Be yourself. Simple and true. Forget trying to be clever witty, hip, whatever. Be relaxed, be present in the moment with your date, don't over-analyze the situation, and the rest will follow. We all want to be the cool guy with the one-liner. Well, I guarantee you that guy never rehearses what he's gonna say before he goes out. That, and he's probably a fictional character with an entire writing staff.

**Don't answer your phone on a date:** Not much to say here, just don't do it. Keeping your phone in your pocket just reinforces to her that she's your only interest at the moment, which is what she wants.

# Planning a Visit to Wellesley College

This seemed important enough to mention. So, Wellesley is one of the most prestigious colleges in the country, just on the edge of Boston that happens to be a women's college. Because of this, a lot of guys in Boston get the impression that it's easy pickings and filled with hot lesbians waiting for a big stud like them to come and make it a threesome. THIS IS NOT THE CASE.

Gentlemen, these are young ladies just like anywhere else. They're smart (smarter than you), and because they're at an all women's school actually means they deserve more respect than you're used to giving to a co-ed, not less, because they're less inclined to put up with your shit. Having dated and befriended several Wellesley ladies, I speak from experience. So here's a few quick tips if you're planning a visit to Wellesley:

1. **Don't go to try and hookup. It won't happen.**
2. **Your normal tactics won't work. Yes, that's right, you're actually going to have to use your brain with these girls.**
3. **That girl you're into could very likely be a lesbian, and no, you're not going to change her mind.**
4. **Treat them like pieces of meat and YOU WILL get slapped and/or kneed in the groin.**
5. **Get a return ticket and know when the last bus leaves, cos you won't be spending the night.**

# A Guide to Modern Etiquette

When I was in 7th grade it was mandatory that the entire grade went to etiquette school. It sucked then, but it's been incredibly useful since, especially in dating. Etiquette is not being a kiss-ass, nor is it for sissies, so don't do it cos you think it'll get you laid. Do it cos it makes you a good date and betters your chances of getting another date. Below are my "rules" to etiquette. Make of them what you will.

1. **Pay attention to your date, follow her lead/cues.** If she likes something, note it. If she doesn't, note it. Apply this to everything over the course of the date.
2. **Hold the door.** Don't make it obvious, but try. Some girls may not like it, in which case you stop (see why rule 1 is important?).
3. **Don't be a pig, whether at the table or in conversation.** At the table, just do everything your mother taught you: Don't chew with your mouth open, use your napkin regularly, etc. In conversation, a little innuendo can be fun if the situation is right, but crude humor and sexist/sexual jokes, not so much. At least not while she's still forming an opinion of you.
4. **Offer to pay. Might be old-fashioned, but still customary.** Whether she says it or not, I guarantee you she's expecting you to at least offer. If she offers to pay then follow the rule of 3. Insist, but if she persists more than twice, go dutch. Again, rule 1.
5. **Mind your manners.** Showing respect for a person is one of the easiest ways to show that you value your date, her time, and her company. It brings down her guard and makes the date that much more enjoyable.

# Advanced Etiquette Techniques

If you really want to try and be a true gentleman, here's a few more guidelines.

- **Wait for your date to sit before you do.**
- **Let her take a bite before you dive in.**
- **Show patience. Whether it's a really old couple blocking the door and taking forever to leave, or poor service at a restaurant, staying cool and in command is an easy way to score points.**
- **Let your date order first. If food is not involved, same principle applies. Ladies first, after all.**

**The Coup-de-Gras:** If she stands to leave the table or is coming back, you should also stand. This is an old-school move, not really practiced today. If she asks what you're doing, just say your momma taught you to, old habits die hard, etc. Kind of amazing how much this can endear you to a girl. That being said, it's all about rule 1., so sense out your date and be as gentlemanly as she's comfortable with.

# Book Legend

Next to each date heading is a quick reference guide to know what the date would entail. It'll look something like this:

## Conversational, $, 1-2-3, Day/Night, Weather

I've tried to keep all the dates around a nice middle ground of relatively inexpensive and not too conversationally focused. I also only focus on the first three dates, because beyond that you can do any of these with your date. Below is a brief legend explaining my method:

**Conversation Light:** The activity is the main focus.
**Conversational:** Aim for a healthy blend of the activity and conversation.
**Conversational Heavy:** The activity is second fiddle to your interaction. **Good luck.**

**FREE = Free**
**$ = $15 or less**
**$$ = $15 to $50**
**$$$ = $50 to $75**

**YOU SHOULD NOT BE SPENDING MORE THAN $75 ON AN EARLY DATE.**

**1-2-3 = This is the date number that I feel that date is appropriate for.**

**1** = Best for a first date, which usually means good for a second or third
**2** = Need at least one date to see if you'd want to do this with them
**3** = Need to know them well enough to know you can spend a lot of time with them.

## 1-2-3 = Good any time.

**Day/Night** = Pretty clear I think, just specifying the ideal time for each date, but not locked in stone. Also, by day I generally mean the afternoon, unless it specifies otherwise.

**Weather** = Just a heads up that you will be spending a decent portion of this date outside, so check the weather and come prepared.

14

# Table of Dates

- Board Games
- Dance Lessons
- Walking Tour
- Esplanade Picnic
- Fenway Park
- Hot Chocolate
- Frog Pond
- MFA Date
- Pumpkin Carving
- Harbor Cruise
- Chinatown
- North End
- Old Theatre
- Rocky Horror
- Shakespeare in the Park
- BSO
- Candlepin Bowling
- Public Transportation
- Foodie Date
- Dinner Date
- Valentine's Day
- Boston Events
- Allston

**Each date will be followed by an info page with fun, useful info for that date.**

# BOARD GAMES
## Conversational,
## $$$,
## 1-2-3,
## Night

Keeping it casual is always a good idea on an early date. That's why the coffee date has persevered as long as it has. But just coffee can get boring and awkward if you have to rely solely on your conversational skills, even for the most cunning linguist.

## Solution: Bring a board game

Simple, really, meet your date at the coffee shop or nearest T stop, wherever, and head inside. Find a table or booth that has some breathing room (you need space to play), order, and then set up.

I suggest bringing your own game as not every place has their own and if they do there's often pieces missing. Bringing your own also shows forethought. Don't worry about "letting her win", just relax and go with the situation. Let the game be a conversation stimulator, not the conversation's focus or limiter. If it's going well, play till you're bored and see where it goes. If it's not, there's no shame in letting a girl beat you. Pay the tab and bail.

# Board Games Info

## Coffee Shops

—      Cafe Luna - Central Sq. (Recommended)

—      Harvard Tea Stop - Harvard Sq.

—      Espresso Royale - BU/Alston

—      Trident Cafe - Back Bay (Recommended)

—      Boston Common Coffee - North End

## Good Games for Conversation

- Bananagrams
- Scrabble
- Pictograms
- Trivial Pursuit

**TIP:** Some games are easy to finish, some take awhile. Regardless of if you finish or not it's really conversation that you're after, so use the game to your advantage. If there are long pauses where you're both focussed on the game, don't be afraid to interrupt it with a question, just make sure it's a leading one and not a yes/no type of question.

# DANCE LESSONS
## Conversation-Light
## FREE,
## 1-2,
## Day/Night

This is a great, locale non-specific date. Don't worry if you're not a great dancer, she won't care (unless she's a dancer) and the exercise will do you good. Well, it'll at least be a fun activity to do together.

Most colleges offer FREE dance classes, you just have to keep your eye out for them. Most are during the day on a weekend, so if it goes well you can still squeeze in a coffee or dinner. Chics like guys who can dance, yes, but they really appreciate a guy who tries, even if he sucks.

**So, Rule no. 76: No excuses, play like a champion.**

# Dance Lesson Info

In case you want to have a little skill before you go to a dance class I've included a basic outline and instruction for your basic East Coast Swing. This is the most basic of the swings, and don't be shy to look online for how-to videos, which are very helpful for learning dance steps.

**EAST COAST SWING:** Known as a triple step swing, the basic count is 1 & 2, 3 & 4, 5, 6.

The pattern is essentially triple step, triple step, rock step.

—    Steps 1 & 2: Triple step to the left (left-right-left)
—    Steps 3 & 4: Triple step to the right (right-left-right)
—    Step 5: Step backwards with your left foot
—    Step 6: Shift your weight to your right foot

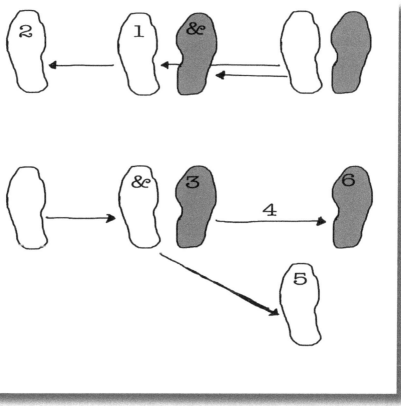

# WALKING TOUR
## Conversational,
## FREE,
## 1-2-3,
## Day or Night,
## Weather

Boston is the walking city, so this one basically writes itself. You're walking a lot on any of the other dates, so why not make a date of it.

**And it's free!**

Here's some suggestions of great places for a stroll. See info page for a list of attractions.

— Beacon Hill
— The Wharfs/Quincy Market
— Harvard, Harvard Sq/ Bank of the Charles
— Freedom Trail
— The Common/Public Gardens
— Esplanade

# Walking Tour Info

## BEACON HILL

— One of the oldest parts of Boston. Classic Boston architecture. Check out Bella Vita for coffee or a snack.

## THE WHARFS / QUINCY MARKET

— The wharfs and the market are both historic parts of old Boston. Quincy Market is great for people watching, and the wharfs offer great views of the harbor. Sitting by Long Wharf at night and watching the planes take off is always a great time.

## HARVARD SQUARE

— Another great place for people watching. Lots of parks, park benches and coffee shops, and the bank of the Charles isn't too far away either.

## FREEDOM TRAIL

— Start in the Common, near Park St. T stop. Get a map from the visitor center if you need to, and then follow the trail. If history's not your thing, just enjoy the walk and your date's company.

## THE COMMON / PUBLIC GARDENS

— No matter the season, the Gardens and the Common are two of the best places for a walk. And if you're looking for something to do, in the spring and summer you have the Swan Boats, and in the winter you've got the Frog Pond. They're quintessential Boston, you can't go wrong.

## ESPLANADE

— My personal favorite spot in Boston. Even with Storrow in sight, between the trees and the bank of the Charles, this is one of the most tranquil and beautiful parts of Boston. Enjoy it while you can.

# ESPLANADE PICNIC

**Conversational,**
**$,**
**2-3,**
**Day,**
**Weather**

Have you ever gotten coffee with someone and then went somewhere else, say a park bench, to be a bit more original? Yeah, you have. We all have. So if you want to vary it up with a little more creativity, here's a suggestion.

For those who do not know, the Esplanade is a gorgeous park running along the Charles from the Mass Ave bridge to the MGH bridge. It's the perfect place for a walk, picnic, etc, and you'd be foolish not to utilize it at some point in your Boston dating career. If it's an early-on date I suggest meeting at Hynes then heading down Newbury a few blocks to Deluca's Market. If it's good weather then screw coffee and pick out a simple picnic. Girls tend to get weird about picnics, so keep it simple and casual. Cheese and crackers, apples/grapes, things like that.

Once you've snacked up head down to the Esplanade, either back up to the Mass Ave entrance or the one off Fairfield. Eat while you walk, or find a nice spot by a tree. If it's bad weather (ie - cold), then perhaps coffee or hot chocolate would be better. In that case, retraction on the whole coffee is lame thing.

# Esplanade Picnic Info

Picnics are tricky things to plan. Like thunder and horses, if it's too much, girls will spook. So here are some safe, simple picnic options that say, "Hey, glad we're spending time together. I'm kind of hungry and need to eat, would you like to eat something too?" Feel free to mix and match based on what you like and what you see.

- Grapes          — Apples
- Pears           — Fresh bread
- Cheese (Cheddar, Gouda, Brie)
- Salami          — Orangina
- Bottled water   — Chocolate

# FENWAY PARK
## Conversation light,
## $$,
## 2-3,
## Day/Night,
## Weather

It wouldn't be Boston without Fenway. This is a must for anyone living in Boston, even if your date's a Yankees fan (especially if she's a Yankees fan!) Games can be pricey, so I recommend a tour instead, which is only about $12/person. Tickets are sold at the team store on Yawkey Way, but they're first-come-first-serve so get there at least 20 minutes before the tour starts. Whether you're a fan or not, there's something magical about Fenway. I suggest going near sunset. Lame as it may sound, the Green Monster is beautiful against the setting sun. I'm a big fan.

To complete the experience get a Fenway Frank. If you're not really feeling food, a happy medium might be going for a quick drink.

# Fenway Park Info

## PHRASES TO SAY THAT MAKE YOU SOUND LIKE A REAL BOSTONIAN

— "Yankees Suck, Yankees Suck!"

— "Jeter drinks wine cool-ahs!"

— "TEDDY FUCKIN' WILLIAMS!"

— Breaking out into the chorus of "Sweet Caroline" at any time

— "A-Rod's prettier than yah sis-tah!"

— "Who won the game last night? Chicago?
It don't fucking matter, Yankees still suck."

# HOT CHOCOLATE
## Conversation heavy,
## $, 1-2-3,
## Day/Night, Weather

It's kind of ironic how so many colleges are in Boston, one of the country's most beautiful cities, yet the majority of the collegiate year is dominated by shitty weather. So how do you plan a date around something as inconvenient and unavoidable as the weather? Two words: Hot Chocolate. Simple, I know, but simple is good. Overdoing it in shitty weather just amplifies it even more, so keep it cool, hot shot.

Here's what you do. On the next page you'll find my recipe for hot chocolate. Now this is not your typical powdered hot cocoa mix. This is the legit shit, the stuff they make over in Switzerland. If it's a first date for you guys then you'll need to make it at home and then meet her at her place or wherever you agree upon. If it's a second or third date, then you can be a bit more bold and invite her over and make it together. Either way, you'll need to end up at the nice part of Comm Ave (where Comm Ave. and Mass Ave. intersect), thermos of hot chocolate in hand.

Since you chose to do this date I'm assuming it's winter or at least fall, so there should be lights in the trees and it should be a really pretty walk. Head towards the Public Gardens, chatting, and passing the hot chocolate between you. Once you get there, well it's your call. If you want to keep it going you can check out some restaurants in that area, see a movie at the Commons theatre, or just improvise.

**Note: Make sure to try this recipe at least once before so you can get it right/tweak it.**

When you call to confirm the date, make sure to tell your date to dress warm and wear comfortable shoes. Don't be that dick in a coat while your girl is shivering in heels.

# Hot Chocolate Recipe

## Ingredients
— Soup pot
— Large bar of Hershey's Chocolate (milk works best but dark is good too!)
— Butter
— Milk
— Patience


## Instructions
— Turn stove to medium-low and let it heat up.
— Once it's hot, put in a 1/4 stick of butter, spreading it evenly around the  pan as it melts.
— Next, put the entire bar of chocolate into the pot without breaking it
— Let the bar get gooey, then add a splash of milk and stir. Don't let it get liquid-y, the milk is just to thicken it up.
— Repeat the previous step until the chocolate is completely melted.
— Stir until smooth and creamy (that's what she said), then pour.

# FROG POND
## Conversation light,
## $-$$,
## 1-2-3,
## Weather

Capitalizing on seasonal things is always a good idea. The idea that the activity is only available at that time can add a little something extra to it. It's like backup.

Nothing's more Boston-in-winter than ice skating at the Frog Pond in the Common. Even with skate rentals it's relatively cheap. It can get busy, so be ready for a possible wait, and bring cash. Don't be the guy who waits half an hour, gets to the front of the line, and has to make his date pay cos he forgot cash.

There's a snack bar there but I recommend either bringing your own winter-themed foods (see Hot Chocolate recipe), or going to Chinatown afterwards for dumplings. It's really hard not to have a good time ice skating, even if you suck, so this is a great winter date. Still, run it by your date before going just in case she had a traumatic ice skating experience as a child.

# Frog Pond Info

## Cost of Admission:
— $4-$8 skate rental

## Hours of Operation:
— M, 10a - 4p     — Tu, 10a - 9p     — W, 10a - 9p
— Th, 10a - 9p     — F, 10a - 10p     — Sa, 10a - 10p
— Su, 10a - 9p

The Boston Common, and the Frog Pond by extension, is one of the oldest city parks in the country, dating back to 1634. It's part of the Emerald Necklace of parks and parkways that extend from the south part of the Common to Franklin Park in Roxbury. Every year from November - March the Frog Pond is open to the public for skating, and in the summer months it's filled with water as a wade pool for kids and families. The Common is considered a jewel of the city, so try and enjoy it as much as possible while you're there.

# MFA DATE
## Conversational,
## $,
## 1-2-3,
## Day

**Generalization:** Chics dig art.
**Equally Broad Generalization:** Chics dig guys who dig art.

Meet your date at the Fenway entrance to the MFA (facing the Fens). Head on in and make sure to bring your student ID (tell your date). Most colleges have a deal with the MFA, so if you're a student chances are it'll be free. But if you're not a student or your date isn't, don't be cheap and offer to pay for your date. If your date is into art then ask leading questions and let her lead. If she's not sure then make a suggestion (check the map), ask the desk, or just wander. Keep it light, point out what you know, point out what you like, and don't be afraid to be goofy and make shit up. If she says anything on a piece, listen, and respond with an open comment so she has more room to talk about her thoughts. People, particularly girls, like to talk about themselves and their thoughts, especially if it makes them seem smart.

When you, or really your date, start to tire of art, head for the museum's cafe. If it's a nice day get some over-priced museum coffee and sit out in the courtyard. If it's not then grab a seat by the window, it's just as good. As always, just let the conversation flow, but you also have the art as backup if need be. You've most likely been talking about art most of the date though, so try and get more into her and what she likes, does, etc. Too much on art seems bland or pretentious.

# MFA Info

## You may not be the biggest art buff, so here's a few suggestions, fun facts, and insights to get you by.

**Tip # 1:** If I mention a piece it's best to familiarize yourself with it before you go.

### — Joseph Turner - The Slave Ship

Gorgeous painting by a British guy depicting the slave trade. Notice the colors, how they move, and the beauty of the setting sun against the ugliness of the body parts in the ocean.

### — The Impressionist Room

More Monet's than any other museum in the world. Everyone knows the "Waterlilies", so mention the "Grainstack (snow effect)" or "Field of Poppies". Also, check out Renoir's "Landscape on the Coast near Menton", my personal favorite. With impressionist paintings remember it's all about what you feel, not what you see. So if you want to say something smart, comment on how the movement of the brush strokes, the texture of the paint (where it's thicker, etc) makes you feel or appeals to you.

**Tip # 2:** If you want to wow your date with some knowledge, here's your coup de grace. The Roger van der Weyden **"St. Luke Madonna"** on the second floor is one of the all time great works of art, and one of the best examples of 15th century Flemish painting. It's full and yet every inch and every depiction serves a purpose. It's still one of the best examples of oil painting, and you can see that in the attention to detail and life-like texture of the fabric behind Mary. As my old art history teacher would say, "... love it." This one is definitely worth researching to have some more info on.

**Tip # 3:** When talking about art, having facts and knowing periods is great, but nothing beats your honest opinion. Combine the two and you'll be golden.

# PUMPKIN CARVING
## Conversational,
## $,
## 1-2-3,
## Day,
## Weather

There's something about carving a pumpkin that's pure, simple fall fun, which is exactly what you're aiming for on this date. Just make sure to do it in either October or November. It's weird any other time. The concept is simple and for simplicity sake I'll base it in Harvard Square, though it's easily adaptable to any other nice part of the city with a place to sit and carve. To start, meet your date at the T stop or some other easily recognizable location. From there head to a grocery store and find yourself a pumpkin. I would say pick up the carving stuff there, but they may not have a kit available, so do a little prep work and have one handy (like one of those kids safety kits with the cool zig-zag cutters and stuff). From the grocers, you'll need to find a place to sit and carve. It's your call, but my suggestion would be the little park near Peet's Coffee off Mt. Auburn St. It's a nice place to sit and talk, you guys can get a cup of coffee/tea/cider/etc, and it's not too far from anything else in the area in case you decide to keep the date going. Which brings us to our next point: if it's going well and she's making it obvious that she wants the date to continue, then suggest dinner. If it's been kind of ..., or you're not sure, then call it on a good note. As far as what to do with the pumpkin... leave it as "street art."

**Tip:** Know where you're going to buy your pumpkin before you meet your date.

# Pumpkin Carving Info

I can't put in a bunch of pictures for copyright reasons, but below are a few ideas to consider. Whatever your idea, try and find/ bring a picture as a guide. Remember, the fun is carving it together, regardless of what it ends up looking like.

The traditional triangle eyes, triangle nose, jagged smile pumpkin, or:
— Any Disney character
— The Citgo sign
— School mascots
— Any current celebrity (I suggest Conan O'Brien)

# HARBOR CRUISE
## Conversational,
## $,
## 2-3,
## Day/Night,
## Weather

Vince Vaughn once said, "Sailing is like sex to these people." One of Boston's best attributes is how close it is to the water. Sometimes it's fun just to get out on a boat. It's a great combination of scenery, activity, and time to talk. Give each one its appropriate balance and you'll have a great date.

There's a few boat options you could take, but here's what I suggest. The boat leaves from Long Wharf, so maybe meet your date at Quincy Market. May not be a bad idea to grab a few snacks while you're there, or bring your own. Once you're good to go head towards the wharf and wait by the MBTA boat dock. I think this goes without saying, but check the times beforehand. You want the boat that goes to Pemberton Point. Roundtrip it should be about an hour and a half and cost about $12 for the two of you. If it's going well, why not get off at Pemberton and take a walk. Just make sure you know when the return boat leaves.

# Harbor Cruise Info

## NAUTICAL TERMS TO KNOW BEFORE BOARDING A BOAT

**Aft =** the back of a ship

**Bow =** the front of a ship

**Port =** the left side of a ship

**Starboard =** the right side of a ship

**Skipper =** the captain

**Futtocks =** Pieces of timber that make up a large transverse frame

**Gunwale =** the upper edge of the hull

**Hull =** the body of the boat

# CHINATOWN DATE
## Conversational,
## $$,
## 1-2-3,
## Day/Night

Chinese food is delicious and comforting, and much like the allure of asian girls on American males, a bit mysterious and intriguing. So of course it's excellent date cuisine. Fairly healthy too for the health conscious and self-conscious of dates. Wherever you choose to meet you'll want to end up at the **Boylston T** stop. The time of day and if it's a weekday or weekend, presents you with a couple of options in Chinatown, so here's a few scenarios.

**WEEKEND DAY-TIME DATE:**
If you find yourself with a date on a Saturday or Sunday during the day, try some dim-sum. Dim-sum is like tapas/appetizers, small portions of one dish that's meant to be shared. It's a lot of fun, allows your to try new things, and share/experience the same things. And it's fairly cheap. I recommend **The Emperor's Garden**, it's an old theatre converted into a restaurant. Classy stuff. So chat it up, impress her with your chopsticks skills, and then get out and explore. If you stick around Chinatown try checking out some of the stereotypical bootleg shops, the Chinatown arch, or as a last resort, see what's playing at the AMC theatre on the Common. If it's a nice day out you may want to head down towards Quincy Market and the wharfs, pick up a little after dim-sum dessert and stroll along the wharfs.

**NIGHT TIME DATE:**
If it's night, try the **Dumpling House.** Anticipate a wait, but they're seriously the best dumplings in Boston. At night you still have the same post meal entertainment options, plus a few more. Check the Wang Theatre for a cool show, as they sometimes have last minute tickets or student tickets* if you want to plan ahead. Or, be adventurous and combine your asian cultures with a bit of Karaoke. What you do is of course up to you and your date, but Chinatown can be a crazy place so have fun with it.* Like the MFA, student tickets are not always for every show, and often given away at a specific time. Make sure to do your prep and call ahead for times and prices.

# Chinatown Date Info

Chinatown has a ton of food options, so I thought I'd list a few more in case you were curious.

— **Windsor Cafe** across from China Pearl has great dim-sum as well, but is a smaller place so it can get crowded pretty easily.

— **Bao Bao Bakery** has some good cookies, cakes, pastries, etc. Located on Harrison under the purple awning.

— **Bubble Tea** is a fun and delicious desert option, and there are some great places in Chinatown. I suggest the little cafe next to China Pearl that's associated with it, but be patient because they make it entirely from scratch.

# NORTH END ADVENTURE
## Conversational,
## $$,
## 1-2-3,
## Day/Night,
## Weather

No matter how many times I go to the North End I still feel like I'm exploring. It's got a vibe unlike any other place in Boston. I definitely recommend a North End adventure at least once in your Boston dating career.

My favorite date was always to meet my date at Haymarket and walk over to the North End. I always enjoy wandering around, checking out menus and spontaneously deciding on a place together. However, your date might be the type who wants you to have a plan, so here's a few suggestions. For lunch, check out Volle Nolle, a great and cheap sandwich place. Bring cash. For dinner you really can't go wrong going with either Bella Vista or Regina Pizzeria. Yeah, Regina is a Boston chain, but this is the original. Great pizza, and a slice (hahaha) of Boston history.

After eating I like to take a stroll through the North End to Copp's Hill Terrace. It's a nice little cove with some benches and a view of the harbor. If you're up for desert and your budget allows, grab some cannolis at Bova's Bakery before you head to Copp's Hill. Mike's is famous but not as good as Bova's and usually has a long line, though it is open later.

The key element of this date is to explore and get the vibe of the North End, and beyond that just go with it.

# North End Info

The North End is rich with history. There's tons of great food, and a lot of cool places to discover, but here are three of the biggest to check out while you're there. Just make sure to find the addresses online before you go.

— **ALL SAINTS WAY:** Hidden away at the end of Hanover St., local Peter Baldassari decorated this alleyway with devotional art to all the saints (hence the name). If you're lucky enough to go on a day when the gate is open and Peter is there, he just might fill you in on who your saint is.

— **THE OLD NORTH CHURCH:** Not to offend anyone, but if you don't know why the Old North Church is a landmark, then what the hell are you doing in Boston? No matter how cliche it may seem, you need to go.

— **PAUL REVERE HOUSE:** Thanks to Boston's great appreciation for history, the house of one of our nation's first heroes is still around today. Walk on by or go inside. History buff or not, it's pretty cool.

# OLD THEATRE DATE
## Conversational,
## $$,
## 1-2-3,
## Night

Boston has some classic, old-school theatre gems hidden all around town. My two favorites are the one in Coolidge Corner and the Somerville Theatre. Dinner and a movie is a little trite. Dinner and a movie in a classic theatre, totally awesome.

Check the times of course. Coolidge shows everything from the newer blockbusters to the classics to Grease sing-alongs. Somerville shows newer films, cult favorites, and occasionally has concerts. You want to be in the main theatre at each place, so call ahead and see what's playing in those rooms.

Coolidge Corner is a great place for a date. Tons of restaurants and it has a 1950's Main street vibe that's a great (first) date atmosphere. After the movie, you're in Brookline so go for a walk. It's one of the best areas for a night time walk.

Somerville Theatre is in Davis Square, an equally cool area. It's really close to Tufts, so lots of student friendly activities and restaurants. You can also try Porter for dinner options since it's just one stop before and has a lot of great restaurants.

Old Theatre Date: classic concept with a retro vibe. Check the next page for some theatre fun facts.

# Old Theatre Info

## — The Somerville Theatre, a History

Built in 1914 and originally part of the Hobbs building, the Somerville Theatre was originally designed for stage shows, vaudeville, opera, and the new art of motion pictures. In 1926, the theatre was purchased by Arthur F. Viano, whose family continued with the theatre's stock theatre troupe until the Great Depression when they were forced into a "movies only" policy in 1932. Maintaining a popular neighborhood presence all through the 30's, 40's, 50's, and 60's, the theatre was known for it's fresh popcorn and gimmicks, such as prize night. The Viano's leased the Somerville to Garen Daly in 1982, who brought live performance back to the stage for the first time since the 30's in the form of live concerts. Daly ran the theatre until 1989 when the building's owners, the Fraiman family, took over and renovated the theatre to it's former glory. Today it's a gem of the Davis Sq. neighborhood, playing first-run movies and regular music and stage performances.

## — Coolidge Corner Theatre, a History

Located in Brookline, the Coolidge Corner Theatre is Boston's only not-for-profit theatre. The building was originally built in 1906 for the Beacon Universalists Church, and was leased to the Harvard Amusement Co. in 1933 to become Brookline's first theatre. As the times changed, the Coolidge was always good to adapt. In the late 70's after an acquisition by Justin Freed, the Coolidge became a showcase for "art" pictures and catered to contemporary tastes for foreign and independent films. Freed later converted the balcony section into another theatre in order to keep up with the burgeoning growth of the modern day multiplex. Eventually Freed decided to sell the theatre, and talks of demolition or conversion into a mall sprung up.

However, the community rallied together in a grassroots campaign to save the theatre. In 1999 the Coolidge Corner underwent a restoration and a rebirth of sorts. Updated with modern comforts, new lighting and carpeting installed, the theatre expanded to include screening rooms for local film makers and a stage for childrens' performances that expanded community programming. A new marquee, installed in 2002, became a symbol of the theatre's significance to the Brookline community, past, present, and future.

# ROCKY HORROR SHOW
## Conversation light,
## $,
## 2-3,
## Night

If your date's a film buff, or just one of those up for anything types, why not test her mettle with the Rocky Horror Picture Show? Who doesn't like sex, drugs, and Tim Curry as a tranny?

It plays sporadically, usually in the fall, so keep your eyes peeled. Coolidge Corner has played it in the past, but I usually see it playing at the AMC in Harvard Sq, and always at Midnight. Oh, and if it's your first time, don't tell anyone. Trust me.

— If you're not familiar with the plot, check the next page for a summary.

# Rocky Horror Info

## THE ROCKY HORROR PICTURE SHOW - SUMMARY

A newly engaged couple are driving home when their car breaks down in the rain. They seek refuge at the castle home of Dr. Frank-N-Furter, a transvestite who just happens to be holding a convention for visitors from the planet Transexual in the galaxy Transylvania. The Doc is set to unveil his latest creation, a young man named Rocky Horror, who was created to give absolute pleasure.

It's a decadent ode to B-movie camp, complete with a soundtrack designed for audience participation. Be ready to go with it, or the audience will turn on you.

# SHAKESPEARE IN THE PARK
## Conversational,
## $,
## 3,
## Night,
## Weather

I confess that I am not the biggest fan of the Bard, but dude has a way with women. Now, one of the best things about living in an expensive city is that it occasionally throws you a bone. Shakespeare on the Common is a rare convergence of these two dating powerhouses. A little arts and culture for her (the Shakespeare), and nothing that's going to bleed you dry in the process (the free part).

There's a few ways you can approach this date. I would suggest loading up on snacks at Deluca's Market on Newbury before heading to the Common. Make sure to get there at least an hour early to find a decent spot. Bring blankets for sitting and cuddling, and cards or a board game for the wait.

What's great about the play being in the Commons is that you can blend it into a number or other dates if it's going well. My top picks would be the Dumpling House in Chinatown, the North End, or Trident back down on Newbury.

— Check the next page for some info and a few Shakespeare fun facts.

# Shakespeare Info

*All the info you'll need for this date can be found at*
*WWW.COMMSHAKES.ORG*

## — SHAKESPEARE FUN FACTS

— Shakespeare never actually published any of his plays

— Shakespeare came from an illiterate family

— Shakespeare married Anne Hathaway. Not the actress.

— No one really knows what the Bard actually looks like, since not one portrait was painted while he was still alive.

— Shakespeare's birthday is unknown but generally celebrated on April 23rd.

— Shakespeare's date of death is also unknown... but is also listed as April 23rd.

# SYMPHONY DATE
## Conversation Light,
## $,
## 2-3,
## Night

Classical music isn't for everyone, so if you really don't like it, don't use this date. Also, don't use this date if you're trying to appear "sophisticated" as your date will totally see right through you. But, if you're a music appreciator and you think your date might be as well, then go for it. And the best part: this date is free (sort of)!

Free, you say? Yes... but here's the rub. In order to make it "free" you'll need a friend... and they'll have to get up early... and so will you. But if you can do that, this could be an awesome date.

The BSO has special student cards that cost $25 and gives you access to a ton of performances for an entire year. All you have to do is show up the morning of the performance you want to see (they list the one's that qualify) and get your ticket. So this is where you'll need a friend. You can only get one ticket per card, and if you want two seats together you'll need to go with your friend to get the tickets. Does this take a bit of planning? Yes. Is it a fun, creative, thoughtful, and totally bad ass date to be sitting in $200 plus seats for free? Fuck yeah it is! So have a great date, and then buy your friend a beer, cos you kind of owe them.

# Symphony Date Info

Below is a diagram of a modern symphony orchestra.   Learn it.

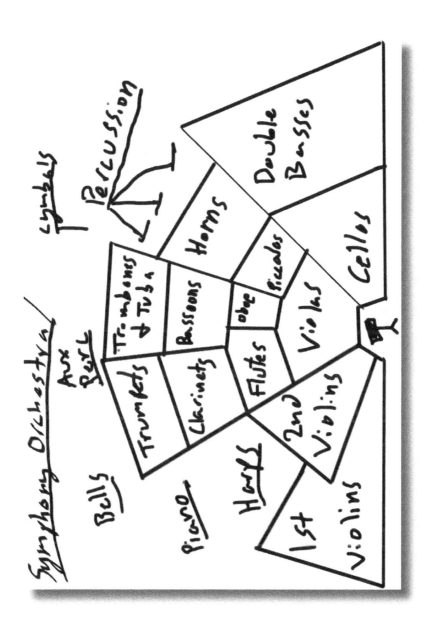

# CANDLEPIN BOWLING
## Conversation Light,
## $,
## 1-2-3,
## Night

Bowling is a classic date. It's great because it's a sport you can play together where no one is expected to be good. Good luck doing that with Racquetball.

Candlepin bowling is even cooler because it's a bizarre take on the concept of bowling. It's an extremely New England activity, originating in Worcester. Essentially the pins are smaller and thinner, like candlesticks, and the balls are small enough to palm (yes, there is a joke here). The rules are also a little different as well.

There's one cool candlepin lane in Davis Sq. that's a little funky, but that's part of it's charm. It's also really close to a great crepe place, Mr. Crepe, that you can take your date to afterwards.

# Rules of Candlepin Bowling

Candlepin is similar to traditional bowling, but there's a few differences worth knowing. Here's a run through on scoring in Candlepin.

— 10 frames, but you roll three times unless you spare/strike, which are called Marks.

— At the end of 3 rolls, the bowler gets credit for the total number of pins knocked down in the frame.

— A spare occurs if all ten pins are knocked down by the first two balls

— A strike only occurs if all ten pins are knocked down with the first ball. For scoring, the bowler gets ten, plus the number of pins knocked down by the next two rolls.

— If there's two consecutive strikes, score 20 in the first frame, 10 in the second, and still total up the number of pins knocked down by the other two balls in each frame.

— 3 strikes in a row: 30 in the first frame, 20 in the second, 10 in the third, and add up the pins from the other two balls in each frame. Any more than three strikes, follow the same pattern.

— Scoring a strike or spare in the 10th frame means that the bowler gets to immediately roll one or two balls as needed to complete the frame.

— Scoring must remain visible to all players at all times. It's the bowler's responsibility to make sure their score is accurate.

**For more info, check out www.bowlcandlepin.com**

# PUBLIC TRANSPORTATION
## Conversational,
## $,
## 2-3,
## Day,
## Weather

Exploring some place you've never been before with someone you don't know that well is a great way to get to know each other and create some quick memories. No matter how long you've lived in the city, there's always still areas left to explore.

Have your date meet you at a T stop that's close to her. Every stop has a map of the whole T system, so find it and pick a station that you hardly ever use, preferably in a part of town you don't get to that often. Then have your date do the same. Buy a ticket for 6 trips and get going.

Each stop you get to head out of the station and find a cool shop or place to go. Parks, independent bookstores, boutique shops, etc. are all ideal. The idea is to explore so just walk around. Give yourself 30-60 minutes in an area just to keep the date moving, then head to your date's pick and repeat. When the date's done take the T back to the station you started at.

*Avoid the known bad areas (sorry Roxbury, Southie) especially at night. Basically, if there's a good reason for you not having gone there, stick to it.*

# Public Transportation Date Info

## My Top 5 T-Stops For This Date

**CLEVELAND CIRCLE**
— Lots of cool shops to explore.

**REVERE BEACH**
— Check out the beach...

**KENDALL or PORTER SQUARE**
— In Kendall check out the Garment District. In Porter, the Porter Exchange.

**BUNKER HILL MONUMENT (COMMUNITY COLLEGE STOP)**
— Head to the Charlestown Navy Yard and check out the Charlestown monument.

**STONY BROOK**
— Get off and take Boylston towards Center St. Check a map to make sure you're going the right way. Tons to do, including visiting the original JP Licks!

# FOODIE DATE
## Conversation Heavy,
## $$,
## 1-2-3,
## Night,
## Weather

— **Scientific fact:** we intrinsically feel closer to those that feed us.
— **More facts:** food releases endorphins and happy brain chemicals.

It's no wonder most dates incorporate something edible. So if you like food (good food), and your date has mentioned liking to cook or trying new restaurants, then this date is for you. Don't worry, it won't break the bank.

Do a little research (or use the list in the back of this book) and pick three nice restaurants, preferably in the same area, or easily accessible via public transportation. Make a game plan of what order to go to them, factoring in things such as peak/rush times, etc. Meet your date near the first restaurant and head over to it. Put in your name, get a table, etc.

Now here's where the date get's cool. Discuss with your date and find one appetizer or small plate and order it to share. That's it! Pay the check and go the next restaurant and repeat. After the third, you can go to your favorite/closest coffee shop and reflect over a little dessert. Or, if you want to continue the theme look up a place that's known for its desserts and order their specialty.

Sampling smaller dishes and hopping from restaurant to restaurant will keep things moving and hopefully give you plenty to talk about.

**Tip:** If you have an iPhone/smartphone use the OpenTable app to make reservations for participating restaurants in advance.

# Foodie Date Info

I can't do all the legwork for you, but here are some of my top suggestions to get you started.

**BACK BAY / FENWAY / KENMORE:**
Petit Robert Bistro
Eastern Standard
Sonsie
Clio

**CAMBRIDGE / SOMERVILLE:**
Ten Tables (there's only ten tables, so factor that in)
Hungry Mother
Craigie on Main
Foundry on Elm

**BEACON HILL:**
Clink (inside the Liberty Hotel)
No. 9 Park

**NORTH END:**
Bricco
Mare

**SOUTH END:**
The Butcher Shop
Gaslight

# DINNER DATE
## Conversation Heavy,
## $,
## 3,
## Night

*\*Avoid as a first/second date, unless you have prior history as friends.*

If you think you've reached a point where you can pull off the dinner date, congrats. How are your cooking skills? Fear not, I got you covered.

How this date goes down is up to you, it's your place. That being said, anytime you have a girl over for dinner the date must have these things (in no order):

An Activity: You can't rely on conversation alone

Good Food: I suggest practicing some meals even when you don't have a date to make sure you can perform under pressure.

*Atmosphere: Don't be corny, skip the playlist. When a girl comes over for dinner she's coming to be entertained and to get a sense of you. So, if you want music put iTunes on shuffle, and clean up but don't cover up.*

When the meal's over, be acutely aware of the vibe. Does she seem engaged and enjoying herself? Then stay in and stay the course. Is she restless or bored looking? Maybe go for a walk or desert somewhere, or walk her home.

Again, this one's all up to you, but I'll help where I can. Flip over for a list of activity and meal suggestions. Good luck.

# Dinner Date Info

## Activities:
— Cooking the meal itself
— Board games
— Browsing your record collection/photographs
— Anything you'd normally do when you're home that you think
   she'd like to share in.

*Avoid watching tv or a movie, unless you invited her over for specifically that reason.

**Food:** Check the recipe section for actual step by step recipes

     — Linguini Alfredo (w or w/o chicken)
     — The Perfect Grilled Cheese
     — Homemade Spinach and Goat Cheese Pizza
     — Southwestern Spaghetti
     — Stuffed Red Peppers
     — Desert Croissant
     — Awesome Avocado Sandwiches

# VALENTINE'S DAY
## Conversational,
## $-$$,
## 1-2-3,
## Night, Weather

So you set a date for Valentine's Day. Stop kicking yourself, it happens. The key is not to avoid the spirit of the holiday, nor to fully embrace it, but to just ride the middle. Acknowledge it, have fun with it, and just don't go overboard on the romance. Treat it like a regular date that happens to be on Valentine's Day. Some of the best and/or most memorable first dates I've had have been on Valentine's Day, so here's what I got.

— Wander around Chinatown and you can find some great deals, like two lobsters for $20 or less. I recommend dinner and a walk through the Common. Guarantee you won't find too many couples spending V-day in Chinatown.

— The MFA puts on a great Valentine's concert (FREE), just check the times.

I call these next few dates "The Down With Love" specials. Instead of playing to the forced romantic nature of the holiday, be the anti-hero. Take her for a decidedly un-romantic date where that's the theme, just make sure to fill her in beforehand.
You could try:

— The "Classy McDonald's" date, or...

— Watch a Rom-Com together, sharing in some booing of all the happy parts, or...

— Go to a coffee shop and make "strictly-platonic-cards-of-formality" for each other.

Avoid the schmaltz, focus on having a good time, and it might just turn out to be one of your best dates.

# Valentine's Day Info

## The Classy McDonald's

Most couples on Valentine's are going to aim for a fancy restaurant or a similar intimate locale. And that's why you're going to go the other route and go to the least fancy, least intimate restaurant in the country: McDonald's. But just going there is something you could do on any date and that'd be really lame. No, you gotta do something that makes going to a shitty fast food restaurant seem really cool. So when you call her to confirm, tell her your plan. You don't have to give everything away, just let her know that you've got something a little untraditional planned. If she's into it, tell her to put on something nice and you'll do the same. Meet her at her place, bring flowers, chocolates, the works. Know where the McDonald's is in her area and plan a nice walk to it. If she lives in Allston or another area that's maybe not the greatest, catch the T to Arlington on the Green Line and walk to the McDonald's on the edge of the Common.

## 3 Cheers for the Anti-Hero

Going to see a romantic comedy is super coupley. Going to see a rom-com and quietly booing the main character while rooting for their enemy or their misfortune is kind of fun, and a cool way to spend the most romantic day of the year with someone you just met. So make plans with your date, dinner, coffee, whatever. Then head to the theatre and sit in the back, quietly snickering to yourselves.

BIG PLUS: If you end up seriously dating this person, you'll have a great "how we met" story and some inside jokes right off the bat.

## Strictly-Platonic-Cards-Of-Formality

This date is a simple twist on the coffee shop date. When you tell your date to meet you for coffee on V-day, she's probably going to be a little disappointed. Whether it's a first date or their 6th Valentine's with the same person, all girls have expectations when it comes to this day. (and a lot of guys too, though we just bottle it up and keep it to ourselves, which is the healthy thing to do). So that's why you're going to have to surprise her when she gets there. Get there ahead of time and pick your table. Have all your gear ready (construction paper, glue sticks, googley eyes, glitter, scissors, etc.).

Order and eat first, and then get to it. Spend the evening talking and making really platonic cards for each other. Here's a few examples:

"You are a pleasant person. I am enjoying your company on this Feb. 14."
— "I hope you have an average day."
— "Thank you for being here... as a friend"
— "That scarf looks nice, and I mean that from a purely platonic, a-sexual place."

# BOSTON EVENTS

One of the best parts of living in Boston are all the things you can only do if you're living there. For these ideas you'll need to research dates and times, but if you happen to have a date during one of these events then you're gold. Feel free to combine with any other date that makes sense (location, time of year, etc.) I'll keep it sparse and informational, since half the fun of these dates are filling them in yourself.

— **Fourth of July:** Christmas in Paris, New Years in Time Square. In my opinion, the Fourth in Boston is right up there in terms of lifetime holiday musts.

*Suggestion: Meet your date around 5 in Central Sq, get coffee/early dinner at Cafe Luna, then walk down to the Cambridge side of the Charles. It's less crowded than the Boston side and just as good of a view. Bring a blanket to sit on.*

— **Boston Marathon:** Generally held towards the end of April and most colleges get the day off. Grab coffee, then find a spot to watch. Bring lawn chairs if you got them.

— **Santa Speedo Run:** An annual event held the second Saturday of every December. Check the deets and find a good place to spectate, or, if you've really adventurous, participate. www.ssrunners.org

— **Restaurant Week:** If you're a foodie, or just want to take your date to nice restaurants, check out Boston's Restaurant Week. It's usually a 3 course prix-fixe affair at participating restaurants in March, and then again in August.

— **Red Sox, Patriots, Bruins parade:** Should you be in Boston right after one of the city's teams wins a championship you've got to check out the parade. Bring snacks, get there early to get a good spot, and go with the fervor. Even if you're not a huge fan, the madness is contagious fun.

— **St. Patrick's Day: Boston.** The Irish. Enough said. Check for parade times, then the rest is up in the air. Don't worry, there's plenty to do.

— **Campus Moviefest:** Held in April at campuses all over the city. It's the largest student film fest in the country. Oh, and it's free.

— **Student Days:** Want to take your date to the Aquarium or Museum of Science but it's a little steep for you? Check the websites and see when the next student day is. You know what makes Penguins even better? Free penguins.

— **Farmers Markets:** Always fun and found all over during the Summer starting May. Might be too coupley for a first date though.

— **Tuesday Night Skate (May):** Bring your own skates and meet at the Hatch Memorial Shell off Storrow. Wrist guards and helmets required, starts at 7.

— **Movies in a Hatch Shell:** Classic Movies every Friday in June. Call 617-227-0627 the day before to find out what's playing.

— **Chowderfest:** Held July 1 and tickets are only $7. Located at City Hall Plaza.

— **Chinese New Year:** Head to Chinatown on Chinese New Year for a crazy time. Check online to see what day it falls on and try to go at night.

— **Latin Nights:** Live bands and free dance instruction every Thursday night in August at Faneuil Hall, 6p-10p.

— **Free NEC Concerts:** Starting the first week of September, NEC puts on free concerts. Free, sophisticated fun without the stuffiness of the BSO. Jordan Hall, 30 Gainsborough St. Call 617-536-2412.

— **Taste of Boston:** Held every September at City Hall Plaza, get a sample of everything local from music, comedy, and local restaurants. Call 617-779-3496 for more info and to check the exact date.

— **Boston Tea-Party Reenactment:** Held Dec. 16, hosted by the Old South Meeting House. It's $1 or free if you come in Colonial costume.

# ALLSTON

Oh Allston... Allston-Rock City. Great for house parties, late nights, and general debauchery. Not so great for dates. So what is my suggestion? Go somewhere else.

Now all you students, before you get all uppity and "fuck you" on me, hear me out. If you're a BU or other student you probably live or spend the majority of your time there. Going on a date should feel new and/or exciting, and a change of scenery can really help.

If you don't live in Allston, here's the rundown in case you were not aware. Allston is the Vegas of Boston, only minus the glitz. It's where you go to get rowdy and maybe do things you wouldn't normally do at home. It has a vibe befitting that, complete with dirty streets, lots of homeless people, and a general rundown facade. Don't get me wrong, it's not without its charm, but not the greatest date environment.

Boston is very easy to get around so I suggest trying any of the other dates in this book. However, if you can't get out of Allston for some reason, attempt the Board Game date, or see if there's a show at the Paradise.

Also, Coolidge Corner, not that far of a walk. Just saying.

# TOOLS FOR DATING IN THE 21ST CENTURY

Every guy needs a wingman. Thanks to the 21st century, you've got one even when you're flying solo. Here are some items I deem necessities for the modern gentleman.

— **Zipcar Membership:** If you're living in the city chances are you don't have a car. This is a great tool to have for any date not in Boston Proper (concerts, hiking, IKEA, etc), or if you just don't feel like taking public transportation.

— **An Umbrella:** I don't think I need to explain why you should already own one of these. My one suggestion would be to have one big enough for two.

— **Coupons:** To some girls this may come off as cheap, but that should just be a sign that they're probably high maintenance and you don't want to date them anyways. This to most women, believe it or not, is an attractive quality. It shows that you plan ahead and value your money. Most schools give out coupon booklets at the start of each semester, so be on the lookout there. Also, sign up for groupon.com, and try retailmenot.com from time to time.

— **Suit:** Not every date has to be a gala, but a good suit is something that every gentleman should have on reserve for any situation. Not a blazer, a suit. Plus, sometimes it's just fun to suit up.

— **Spare T card:** Say your date forgets her T card, or yours gets tapped out and you don't have enough on your debit to cover it. No problem, just keep a spare T card for $20 tucked away in your wallet. Make sure to get the ticket and not another CharlieCard, otherwise the gate sensor will get confused.

— **Cash:** You never know when you're gonna need it. Ninety percent of the time your card'll do fine, but nothing worse than being at a restaurant and finding out it's cash-only after you've eaten. Just grab a $20 out of the ATM on your way to meet your date just in case.

— **Board Game(s):** Notice how a board game is a great backup activity and how I mention it in several dates? Yeah, you should go buy one.

*Most of us have an iPhone or smartphone these days, so these next couple are great apps to have on hand for a date.*

— **Open Table:** The restaurant you wanted to go to is closed? Waited till the last minute and just found out the place you want to go to is reservation only? Don't sweat it. Download the OpenTable app and you'll be fine. OpenTable shows you all the restaurants in your area and their reservation availability in real time. Handy.

— **Save Me:** Should you find yourself on a date where you really need to bail, this is your best friend. Open the app, tell it how many seconds to wait, and then it'll fake call you. You can pretend it's an emergency, politely say goodbye, and get out, dignity intact.

— **Flixster:** This handy app shows you all the theaters near you, as well as lists what they're showing and the times.

— **The Weather Channel:** This app's a no-brainer. If your date says it's gonna get bad later, you can see when it's supposed to and adjust your date around that. You can't control the weather, but you can avoid being caught out in the rain.

# RESTAURANT LIST

So this isn't exactly Zagat or Urbanspoon, but here are the restaurants that I mention throughout the book and a few others worth knowing.

## Back Bay / Fenway

— **Trattoria Toscana** - Best Italian food outside the North End! Very few tables and no reservations, so be ready for a possible wait.

— **Hsin Hsin Cafe** - Best Chinese in the Back Bay.

— **Robert Petit Bistro** - Slightly pricy, but excellent French cuisine.

— **Deluca's Market** - This market is a little over priced on some things, but the humongous deli style sandwiches are a great deal.

— **Parish Cafe** - On Boylston at the edge of the Public Gardens, amazing food, great atmosphere, fair price.

## Central Square

— **Cafe Luna** - My all time favorite place in Boston. All the food is amazing, especially the paninis. The deserts are wonderful, and hands down the best baristas in Boston. There's free music nearly every night, and you can sit outside in good weather. For lunch, dinner, or brunch, you can't beat it. Tell them Adrien sent you.

— **Toscanini's** - Boston is plentiful on good ice cream places, but Toscanini's takes the cake for quality and flavor.

— **Hungry Mother** - The best Southern Food in all of Massachusetts! It's pricier than most of the places I mention, but one of the best restaurant experiences you can have.

# Harvard

— **Mr. Bartley's Burger Cottage** - Some of the best burgers in all of Boston. This place is a must at least once while you're in Boston.

— **Arrow St. Crepes** - Serving both savory and desert crepes, this is a near perfect date place. Starred items are student discountable! Discounts are supposedly just for Harvard students, but just try it.

— **The Boston Tea Stop** - Clever name, huh? They only serve bubble tea, which can be a fun desert.

— **Veggie Planet** - Part of Club Passim, a Cambridge landmark. Great place if you're out with a vegetarian, and it tastes good enough you won't mind.

## Porter and Davis Squares

— **Kaya House (Porter)** - Korean barbecue is absolutely delicious and this place is the best. Authentic and tasty. If you don't know what stuff is, be adventurous!

— **Red Bones Barbecue (Davis)** - While it may seem a bit messy for a date, barbecue is actually great date food. It's hard to find good barbecue this far north, but Redbone's has got it.

— **Martsa on Elm - (Davis)** - Great, cheap asian grub.

— **Christopher's - (Porter)** - American bar food may seem generic for a date, but not if it's done right. This is done right.

— **Mr. Crepe - (Davis)** - Crepes on a date, you really can't go wrong. Simple, elegant, and delicious. Says refined, yet fun, all in one breath.

# North End

— **Giacomo's -** This one was recommended to me via my Wellesley ladies. If it's good enough for them, it's good enough for you.

— **Volle Nolle -** Best sandwiches in the North End. Cash Only.

— **Regina Pizzeria -** The original pizzeria that spawned the rest of the well known Boston chain. It's a popular place, but the pizza is well worth the wait.

— **Bella Vista -** My personal favorite sit-down italian place in the North End. There's a lot of great options though, so just browse around.

— **Bova's Bakery -** Mike's is the famous one, but this is the best.

## Beacon Hill / Faneuil Hall

— **Durgin Park -** One of the oldest restaurant's in Boston. Classic New England fare, especially their Pot Roast and their famous Indian Pudding.

— **Dick's Last Resort -** The waitresses are supposed to give you a hard time, so it may not seem like the ideal place. However, if you're date is a good sport, it's a good Boston experience.

— **Quincy Market Food Court -** May seem kind of cheap and lame, but playing tourists and having tons of options can be fun. You can make an activity of trying every sample.

— **Bella Vita -** Nestled at the foot of Beacon Hill, just off the Commons on Charles St. Great little cafe for coffee or ice cream.

# Chinatown

— **The Emperor's Garden** - An old theatre converted into a restaurant. Serves Dim-sum on weekends during lunch hours.

— **Dumpling House** - Best. Dumplings. In. Boston. Go.

— **Windsor Cafe** - Also a great place for dim-sum, but it's smaller so it fills up quickly.

— **Bao Bao Bakery** - A great little desert place that makes an awesome bubble tea.

*See the Foodie Date info page for high end ($$$$) suggestions.

# RECIPES

## Linguini Alfredo

### Ingredients
— Fresh linguini (get at grocery store)
— Olive oil
— Butter
— Heavy Cream
— Grated Provolone and Parmesan

— 1. Bring water ( a little over half mark of pan, in this case) to a rapid boil.

— 2. Add 1 Tablespoon of olive oil, a pinch of salt and the linguini (fresh pasta cooks in 2-3 minutes, otherwise follow package directions).

— 3. Drain and cover when done to keep pasta hot.

— 4. Using the same pan (which is still hot), over medium heat add 1/2 teaspoons olive oil to 2 Tablespoons butter, if butter starts to sizzle, lower heat lightly, add 1/4 cup heavy cream, season with a dash of salt and pepper, stir and heat it to thicken a bit (about 2 minutes), you'll see steam rising. Do not boil.

— 5. Return pasta to pan, turn off heat, add grated provolone and parmesan cheese, toss and serve immediately.

— If you're going to add chicken, follow the next recipe.

# RECIPES

## Pan Seared Chicken with Mushrooms

### Ingredients
— Package of boneless chicken breasts (I prefer thin sliced)
— Onions
— Mushrooms
— Olive Oil

— 1. Season chicken breasts with herbs, garlic, pepper, dust with flour.

— 2. 1/2 cup of chopped or sliced onions.

— 3. 5/6 medium size mushrooms sliced.

— 4. Heat skillet on high, add olive oil , reduce to medium, add onions.

— 5. Add chicken, flip after 2 minutes, add mushrooms, salt if desired. Lower heat a little and cook for another 3/4 minutes. Cover when done.

— Should take about 6-8 minutes of cooking time. Let rest for a few minutes after cooking.

# RECIPES

## Stuffed Red Peppers

### Ingredients
— 2 or more large red peppers
— Pepper Jack cheese
— McCormack Mesquite seasoning
— 1 medium to large onion
— Dill herb
— Ritz Crackers

— 1. Preheat oven to 450°.

— 2. Slice off the top of the pepper, cut out the ventricles.

— 3. Mash up several Ritz crackers, make as fine as possible.

— 4. Mix cracker crumbs with Mesquite seasoning.

— 5. Chop half the onion into small pieces.

— 6. Fill each half of the pepper with onion, then a little cheese, then a layer of cracker crumbs, cover with layer of cheese.

— 7. Pack each half full, put in the oven and let bake for 15 minutes.

— 8. Serve immediately.

# RECIPES

## Homemade Spinach and Goat Cheese Pizza

### Ingredients
— Whole wheat/ whole grain pizza dough
— 1 small log of goat cheese
— 1 nice tomato
— Spinach
— 1 yellow onion
— Butter
— Olive Oil
— Anything else you want to add! Cause its pizza.

— 1. Grease your pan and stretch your dough, and set the oven to 400°.

— 2. First, caramelize the onions. This is not scary, but it takes a while, so do it first. Cut the onion lengthwise, any thickness is fine (that's what she said), and place them in a small pan with some butter and/or oil. Let cook for about 30 minutes, stirring every so often until they're brown.

— 3. Put just the stretched dough in the oven for about 3-4 minutes.

— 4. Once you take out the dough, put about a quarter of your goat cheese on the pizza. It will melt better if the dough is still hot.

— 5. Slice your tomato, put it on the pizza.

— 6. Lightly (as in barely) steam your spinach, and then mix with the remaining goat cheese. Spread on pizza.

— 7. Caramelized onions (when they are done) go on last.

— 8. Cook for 12-13 minutes, or until it looks ready.

*Recipe courtesy of Ms. Kirsten McNally.*

# RECIPES

## Southwestern Spaghetti

---

### Ingredients
— Spaghetti
— 1lb package of chicken breast (I like thin sliced, cooks faster)
— McCormack Mesquite seasoning
— Tabasco
— Onion
— Olive oil

— 1. Boil water, once ready, add spaghetti.

— 2. While water is boiling take out chicken breasts, coat each side with mesquite seasoning.

— 3. Heat up pan, coat with olive oil, and when ready cook chicken and onion.

— 4. Make sure to check on your spaghetti.

— 5. As chicken is still cooking, drain spaghetti, then remove the chicken from the pan.

— 6. Once spaghetti is drained, add olive oil to the pan used for cooking the chicken, then throw spaghetti in that pan and sauté it.

— 7. After spaghetti is sautéed a little, add 6-8 dashes of Tabasco to the pasta.

— 8. Mix in tabasco and sautéed spaghetti until some is slightly blackened.

— 9. Put spaghetti on plates, put chicken breasts on top, and serve!

# RECIPES

## Perfect Grilled Cheese

### Ingredients
— Bread (I prefer fresh baked wheat)
— American Cheese
— Butter

— 1. Melt an 1/8 stick butter in the pan on light-medium heat.

— 2. Coat the outsides of each piece of bread in melted butter. Let it absorb into the bread.

— 3. Put on 2 slices of American cheese on one piece of bread.

— 4. Place other piece on top, and then flip so that the piece you just placed on top is now on the pan.

— 5. Repeat flipping, 30 seconds to a side, until crispy and golden brown.

*** *This is a simple, delicious meal. The grilled cheese being such a childhood staple, can really take the pressure off a dinner date and help the two of you relax. Just make sure to pair it with a salad, or at least something to contrast the greasy, gooey goodness.*

# RECIPES

## Awesome Avocado Sandwiches

---

### Ingredients
— Bread or Bagels (plain or everything)
— Chive Cream Cheese
— Smoked Salmon (pre-packed at grocery store) or Eggs
— One ripe Avocado

— 1. Toast your bagels (or bread).

— 2. Peel and slice your avocado into thin strips, but not too thin.

— 3. If you're making the egg version, go ahead and fry two eggs (one for each of you). Don't be stingy with the butter, as it gives the eggs an extra crunch when frying. If not, the smoked salmon should be ready to go.

— 4. Coat your bagels liberally with the chive cream cheese. Ask your date how much she likes, of course.

— 5. Then assemble. It should go: bagel, cream cheese, avocado, egg or salmon, bagel.

*The egg version is great for breakfast, or breakfast-for-dinner, and the salmon version is good anytime, especially for picnics.*

# RECIPES

## Hot Chocolate

---

### Ingredients
— Soup pot
— Large bar of Hershey's Chocolate
(milk works best but dark is good too!)
— Butter
— Milk
— Patience

— 1. Turn stove to medium-low and let it heat up.

— 2. Once it's hot, put in a 1/4 stick of butter, spreading it evenly around the pan as it melts.

— 3. Next, put the entire bar of chocolate into the pot without breaking it.

— 4. Let the bar get gooey, then add a splash of milk and stir. Don't let it get liquid-y, the milk is just to thicken it up.

— 5. Repeat the previous step until the chocolate is completely melted.

— 6. Stir until smooth and creamy (that's what she said), then pour.

# RECIPES

## Desert Croissant

### Ingredients
— 1 Croissant (from a real bakery)
— Granny Smith Apple
— Brie Cheese
— Honey
— Crushed Almonds

— 1. Preheat oven to 350° or you can use a toaster oven.

— 2. Slice granny smith apple in half, then into thin slices.

— 3. Cut the brie into thin slices.

— 4. Cut the croissant in half, then put the apple slices in a single layer on both halves, put a slice of brie on top of each apple slice, then put in oven.

— 5. Let bake for 5-7 minutes, or until brie is slightly melted and croissant is nicely toasted.

— 6. Take out of oven, drizzle with honey, then sprinkle the crushed almonds on top.

— 7. Serve right away.

*Special thanks to Wellesley's Hoop Café.*

# NOTES

# NOTES